ZEN COMICS

Compiled and Drawn

by

IOANNA SALAJAN

CHARLES E. TUTTLE COMPANY
Rutland Vermont   Tokyo Japan

copyright 1974

Published by the Charles E. Tuttle Co., Inc., of Rutland, Vermont &
Tokyo, Japan; with editorial offices at Suido 1-chome, 2–6, Bunkyo-ku,
Tokyo, Copyright in Japan, 1974, by Ioanna Salajan. All rights reserved.

Library of Congress Catalog Card No. 74–35679. International Standard
Book No. 0-8048 1120-2. Sixteenth printing, 1994. PRINTED IN SINGAPORE

to Richard

ZEN COMICS

①

②

ZEN COMICS

③

④

Zen Comics

⑤

Dear Master, dear master, it has finally come to me; all is nothing; all is emptiness!

There is no me, no you, no thing!

Even a good thing isn't
as good as no thing.

⑥

⑦

Here is a large rock. Do you think it's inside or outside your mind?

(ahem) Well from the Buddhist point of view all things are an objectification of the mind, so, I would say this rock is inside my mind.

Well, if you're carrying a thing like that in your mind, your head must be very heavy!

Zen Comics

⑧

⑨

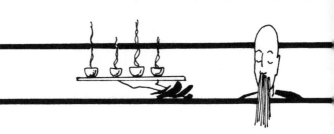

ZEN COMICS

⑩

ZEN COMIX

⑪

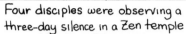

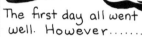

⑬

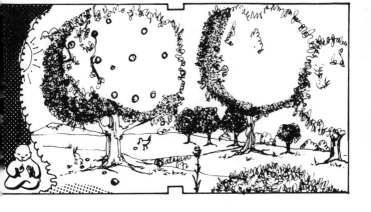

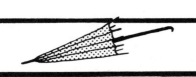

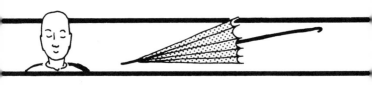

5 hours later

nitefall

Master, isn't it that we monks are to keep ourselves free from contact with women?

I left the girl at the riverside; are you still carrying her?

ZEN COMICS

Nothing is left
for you at
this moment
but to laugh.

ZEN COMICS

ZEN COMICS

⑯

17

Master, if I don't have anything in my mind, what shall I do?

Throw it out!

But if I don't have anything, how can I throw it out?

Well, then CARRY it out!

⑱

⑲

20

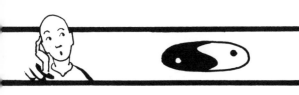

㉑

when sitting
just sit

when walking just walk

Above all
don't wobble

㉒

zen comics

23

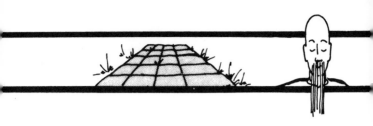

㉕

When the ordinary man attains
Knowledge he's a sage,
When the sage attains
understanding he's
an ordinary man.

26

28

(29)

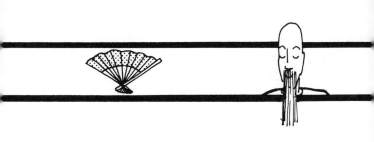

ZEN COMICS

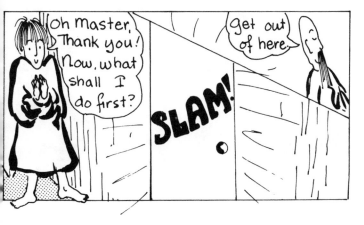

ZEN COMICS

(31)

(32)

ZEN COMICS

(33)

Master, what is my Self?

What would you want with a Self?

What was your
   face before your
   parents were born?

34.

ZEN COMICS

(35)

It's the custom to make and win an argument abou

the Buddha to gain a nite's lodging in a Zen temple.

LATER What a wonderful fellow your brother is!

?!

He completely defeated me!

Oh really? Tell me about it.

Well first I held up one finger — Buddha the enlightened one.

First he held up one finger, making fun of my one eye!

Then to teach *him* to be polite, I held up two fingers—happy he had two eyes.

Then that guy holds up *three* fingers—meaning we only have three eyes between us!

I got so angry. I shook my fist in his face & he got scared & ran away!

Working hard
Accomplishing
No-thing.

(36)

37

Master, why don't you have a picture of the perfect Buddha?

I do. Right behind that curtain.

ZEN COMICS

38

Zen Comics

40

A fallen blossom.
Come back to its branch?
No, a butterfly!

[Moritake (1452-1549)]

(41)

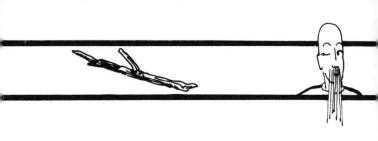

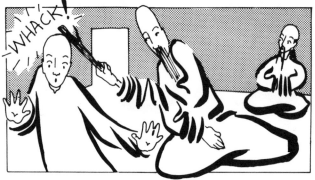

42

(43)

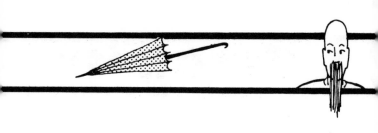

Zen comics

Zen Comics

ZEN COMICS

㊻

ZEN COMICS